8TH GRADE
ENGLISH AND LANGUAGE ARTS
Unit 9
Speaking, Listening, and Viewing

Y0-DBV-872

Table of Contents

Leadership 101

DISCERNMENT

Understanding the deeper reasons why things happen

ResponsiveEd thanks Character First (www.characterfirst.com) for permission to integrate its character resources into this Unit.

Objectives

- Understand the purposes of various types of media.

- Analyze how words, images, graphics, and sounds work together in various forms to impact meaning.

- Interpret how visual and sound techniques influence the message.

- Evaluate the role of media in focusing attention on events and informing opinion on issues.

- Evaluate various techniques used to create a point of view in media.

- Evaluate the impact of media on the audience.

- Understand the use of propaganda techniques in media.

- Assess the correct level of formality and tone for successful participation in digital media.

- Use comprehension skills to listen attentively to others in formal and informal settings.

- Follow and give complex oral instructions to perform specific tasks, answer questions, or solve problems.

- Summarize formal and informal presentations.

- Speak clearly and to the point, using the conventions of language.

- Use eye contact, speaking rate, volume, enunciation, a variety of natural gestures, and conventions of language to communicate ideas effectively.

- Advocate a position using anecdotes, analogies, and/or illustrations.

- Work productively with others in teams.

- Participate productively in discussions, plan agendas with clear goals and deadlines, set time limits for speakers, take notes, and vote on key issues.

WHAT IS DISCERNMENT?

Most of an iceberg is below the surface, so it takes discernment to know where a ship can safely pass. It also takes discernment to figure out what to do and where to go in life.

A discerning person asks questions in order to find answers. "Why did this happen?" "Does this happen often?" "When did it start?" "Why did it stop?" "What happened next?" Use your mind to solve problems and avoid needless mistakes.

1. MEDIA BASICS

Objectives:

- Understand the purposes of various types of media.
- Analyze how words, images, graphics, and sounds work together in various forms to impact meaning.

Vocabulary:

media – means of communication intended to reach or influence a large audience

target audience – the specific group of people at which a media message is aimed

CHARACTERISTICS OF MEDIA

Have you ever formed an opinion about a product based on a television commercial? Perhaps you watched a commercial for athletic shoes, and you immediately felt that you had to have them. Or maybe a commercial advertising a type of candy bar or sports drink gave you an instant craving. Television commercials are often very adept at causing an audience to feel or think a certain way.

In the previous Unit, you studied persuasive writing and speaking. You learned about persuasive techniques, such as appeal to logic or emotion, which are intended to influence an audience's thoughts or actions. You also examined persuasive elements in speeches and essays. In this Unit, you will look at different types of media and examine how media messages influence the opinions and actions of particular audiences.

Media forms—billboards, television, news-papers, magazines, radio programs, movies, websites—are all around you. As you take in the images and messages that surround you, it is important that you understand that each one is designed for a specific purpose. The word **media** is used to refer to means of communication intended to reach or influence a large audience. The definition implies that media messages have the purpose of persuading a large audience. Many people allow media to influence them without thinking about the messages presented.

Let the joy bubble.

Radiant.
Refreshed.
Ready to go.

Example 1.1

BASIC PRINCIPLES OF MEDIA:

- Media messages are *always* constructed with a purpose. They are designed by a person to accomplish a specific effect. Usually, the purpose of a media message is to persuade the audience to do something. Often, media messages attempt to shape the audience's beliefs, values, and opinions. The first step to understanding media messages is realizing that each message and image has a specific purpose.

- Media messages are shaped by graphics, sound, pictures, and text features. Rather than using only words, as in a persuasive essay, media messages combine text with other elements designed to attract a wide audience.

- Media messages are usually intended for a specific group of people, the **target audience**. For example, a billboard advertising a children's museum is aimed at capturing the attention of children and families with young children. Members of a target audience share certain characteristics, such as age, gender, interests, values, or ethnicity.

- Media messages present underlying values, beliefs, and points of view that the audience is supposed to adopt. In the example of a billboard advertising a children's museum, the billboard's purpose is to persuade the family to visit the museum. In addition to a persuasive message, the billboard may present the idea that families need to spend more time together and that visiting the museum will make their children smarter. Look for hidden values or points of view presented by media messages.

- Media messages are usually distributed for the purpose of gaining profit or power. Messages often present a product that, if purchased by a large number of people, will bring a large profit to a company. Messages can also promote a person, such as a candidate seeking a political office.

Look at the image in **Example 1.1**. What message does the advertisement present? What underlying value or point of view does it contain?

The advertisement is obviously attempting to persuade an audience to buy the brand of soft drink advertised. The advertisement also suggests that you will feel happy and have more energy if you purchase this soft drink. Do you see the persuasive message as well as the underlying message? How does the advertisement accomplish its purpose? It uses a combination of text, graphics, and color to send the message that if you drink this soft drink, you will be happy and energetic. The advertisement promotes a product as well as a particular lifestyle and set of values. Is the message true? Will drinking this soft drink bring you happiness? Asking yourself these questions will help you to determine the validity of the persuasive message that is communicated.

PURPOSES OF MEDIA

A media message usually has a main purpose, or reason, for being delivered. Sometimes, the purpose can be two-fold, as in a commercial that makes the audience laugh but also convinces them to purchase a product. Following are the primary purposes of media messages.

- **Inform** – Media products that have the main purpose of informing the audience include news articles and broadcasts, public service announcements, sports broadcasts, and some websites.
- **Entertain** – Examples of media products that are designed to entertain include television shows, movies, music recordings, and video games.
- **Persuade** – Many media messages have the explicit or underlying purpose of influencing an audience. Some persuasive media products include advertisements, movie and book reviews, political commercials, and editorials.

TYPES OF MEDIA:

As you learned earlier in this Lesson, the word *media* refers to a means of communication intended to reach a large audience. Some means of communication include newspapers, television, radio, billboards, magazines, and the Internet. Each of these is a *medium* (singular form of *media*), a method of spreading informational, persuasive, or entertaining messages.

- **News** – News media include current events in magazines and newspapers, television and radio news broadcasts, and Internet news articles. News media messages are primarily intended to inform audiences, but they can also entertain. News media present factual information, but they can contain bias and inaccurate information.
- **Television shows** – Television shows include sitcoms, dramas, reality shows, talk shows, and informational shows. Most television shows are designed to entertain, but some inform as well. Television shows employ camera techniques and use sound to enhance the entertainment. Television shows are supported by companies who advertise their products during commercial breaks.
- **Advertising** – Advertising can come in many forms, including television and radio commercials, billboards, signs, newspaper and magazine advertisements, mailings, and Internet advertisements. They are designed to attract a target audience, and they use graphics, images, sound, and text to send a persuasive message.
- **Websites** – Websites can have the purpose of entertaining, persuading, or informing. They present information in the

form of text, graphics, images, sound, animation, and video.

- **Feature films** – Feature films include movies, which are produced for the purpose of entertaining an audience and gaining a profit. Movies tell fictional or nonfictional stories and use actors, sets, props, music, cinematography, and special effects to entertain an audience. Some feature films, such as documentaries, have the purpose of informing or persuading an audience.

With all the different types of media, it is difficult to escape its influence. Media messages are everywhere. As you take in the messages that surround you, try to discern the explicit intent and underlying purpose of each one. Understanding the purpose of a media message will help you to resist being influenced or persuaded by it. Keep in mind the main purpose of most media messages—to make money or gain power. Also, seek to understand the values and beliefs communicated by the media messages that you receive.

 **Review**

Write the correct answers.

1.1) What is the definition of *media*? _____

_____

1.2) List five types of media.

a. _____   d. _____

b. _____   e. _____

c. _____

1.3) Media messages are always constructed with a(n) _____ .

1.4) Media messages are shaped by _____, _____,

_____, and _____ _____ .

1.5) Media messages are usually intended for a specific group of people, the _____

_____ .

1.6) Media messages present underlying _____, _____,

and _____ _____ _____ that the audience is supposed to adopt.

1.7) Media messages are usually distributed for the purpose of gaining _____

or _____ .

4

Match each type of media with its _primary_ purpose. Answers will be used more than once.

1.8) _____ newspaper article

1.9) _____ television sitcom

1.10) _____ documentary

1.11) _____ billboard advertisement

1.12) _____ animated movie

1.13) _____ website about skateboarding

1.14) _____ commercial for a vacation destination

1.15) _____ radio news broadcast

1.16) _____ talk show

1.17) _____ advertisement for a candy bar

A. entertain

B. inform

C. persuade

Advertisement Activity

Find a print advertisement in a newspaper or magazine. Answer the questions about the ad and bring it to class.

1.18) Where did you find the ad? _____

_____

1.19) What company is responsible for the ad? (Hint: Look for a logo—a symbol used by companies

to identify their products.) _____

_____

1.20) What is the ad trying to get you to do, buy, or think? _____

_____

1.21) Who is the target audience of this ad? What makes you think so?_____

_____

_____

1.22) What do you think of the ad? Does it make you want to purchase the product? _____

Why or why not?_____

_____

Teacher Check

2. ELEMENTS OF MEDIA

Objectives:

- Analyze how words, images, graphics, and sounds work together in various forms to impact meaning.
- Interpret how visual and sound techniques influence the message.

Vocabulary:

camera angle – the position of a camera while it is taking a shot

close-up shot – allows the audience to see a person's facial expression and helps create a certain emotion

graphic elements – elements such as font size and type that contribute to the media message

high-angle shot – a camera angled down at its subject

long shot – shows the subject and its surroundings, allowing the audience to see the "big picture"

low-angle shot – a camera pointed up toward its subject

sound techniques – sound effects, music, and voice-overs; used in film, radio, and television to affect and enhance meaning

special effects – computer-generated images and manipulated images that create an illusion

visual techniques – elements, such as camera angles and lighting, that influence the message

6

As you learned in Lesson 1, media messages are designed for a specific purpose—to entertain, persuade, or inform. Images, text, graphics, and sound enhance the message presented and can be used to make the audience think or feel a certain way. Often, graphics, images, and sound present a clearer message than the text itself does. For example, scary music in a movie gives the audience a clue that something bad is about to happen. The audience is able to understand the impending action based on the background music.

VISUAL TECHNIQUES

Media messages employ **visual techniques** to enhance the message. Visual techniques include camera angles, lighting, and effects such as color, lines, shape, and special effects. In film and television, a **camera angle** is the position of the camera while it is taking a shot. A camera angle creates a certain effect. For example, a camera angle pointed up toward its subject (**low-angle shot**) causes the subject to seem more imposing or threatening, while a camera angled down at its subject (**high-angle shot**) makes the subject seem weak or vulnerable. A **close-up shot** allows the audience to see a person's facial expression and helps create a certain emotion. A **long shot** shows the subject and its surroundings, allowing the audience to see the "big picture."

Lighting is another visual technique used in media. The light in an image focuses the audience's attention on a specific point. Bright lights create a happy, cheerful mood, while darkness and shadows can create a mood of sadness or mystery. Lighting is used intentionally to enhance a media message.

High-angle shot

Low-angle shot

Color is also used to achieve a certain effect. Colors can highlight certain elements of the text, or they can create a specific mood, such as happiness, sadness, calmness, or peace. Warm colors, like red, orange, and yellow, can convey a mood of happiness or excitement. Cool colors, like blue and green, can contribute to a melancholy or calm mood.

Lines and shapes help focus the audience's attention on certain elements of the message by pointing toward an object or shape. Lines can create a feeling of depth or motion, and they can help emphasize the subject. Shapes are outlines of objects, and they can be used to symbolize or emphasize objects or ideas.

In the following picture of a car advertisement, notice how shapes are used for representation. The "greater than" sign means "better than" or "stronger than," and the shapes represent dangerous driving conditions. The message is conveyed by shapes and images.

Car advertisement

Special effects, manipulated images and graphics, are used to create a certain illusion. Fast-motion sequences in film and television make a scene seem more exciting, while slow-motion sequences intensify the drama of a scene. Special effects can be used to simulate imaginary events or objects, such as disasters or imaginary creatures, and make them seem realistic.

SOUND TECHNIQUES

Media creators use **sound techniques**, such as sound effects, music, and voice-overs, to affect and enhance meaning in television, film, and radio. Sound techniques can create mood, enhance action, or emphasize story elements. Sound effects are sounds added to films, television and radio programs, or commercials. Sounds like laughter, animal sounds, and punches in a fight scene help to entertain an audience and make a scene more realistic.

Background music plays an important role in television, film, and radio. Music often sets the mood of a scene and can affect the audience's feelings. Music can create moods such as excitement, suspense, sadness, joy, or calmness. For example, the background music for a police chase scene would be fast-paced and exciting, while the music for a scene picturing two friends casually riding bicycles through a shaded park would be calm and peaceful.

A voice-over is the voice of an unseen narrator or commentator in a television show, commercial, movie, or radio show. Narrators and commentators are selected for having a certain quality of voice. For example, a sports commentator usually has a dramatic, commanding voice, adding to the excitement of the game. In contrast, a person doing a voice-over for a commercial for infant formula would probably have a soft, pleasant, calming voice.

GRAPHIC ELEMENTS

Graphic elements, such as headlines and sizes and styles of fonts, are visual or text elements used to emphasize a media message. Headlines are designed to capture an audience's attention, so advertisers usually try to use eye-catching fonts and interesting wording. Other graphic elements, such as charts, graphs, and tables, can enhance and clarify a media message by providing information in an easy-to-read format.

When you evaluate media messages, look for visual and sound techniques and graphic elements. Determine whether these elements enhance, detract from, or hide the intended message.

Review

Write the correct answers.

2.1) What are six visual techniques/effects that media producers use to enhance media messages?

a. _____ d. _____

b. _____ e. _____

c. _____ f. _____

2.2) Explain how camera angles can affect how a subject is perceived. _____

_____

_____

_____

2.3) What are three sound techniques that media producers use to enhance media messages?

a. _____ c. _____

b. _____

2.4) What are graphic elements? _____

_____

_____

Study the following photograph; then, answer the questions based on your analysis.

This photograph was taken by Lewis Hine, a man who worked as a photographer for the National Child Labor Committee. He was hired to photograph children working in mills to spread awareness about the injustices of child labor.

2.5) What kind of shot or angle is used in the photograph? _____ _____

2.6) How does the shot or angle enhance the message of the photograph? _____

_____

_____

2.7) How does lighting enhance the mood of the photograph? _____

_____

_____

2.8) Where do the lines in the photograph point? _____

_____

_____

2.9) How do lines enhance the photograph? _____

_____

_____

2.10) What is the overall message of the photograph? (Hint: Look at the photograph description.)

_____

_____

Define the terms.

2.11) special effects – _____

_____

2.12) long shot – _____

_____

2.13) close-up shot – _____

_____

2.14) low-angle shot – _____

_____

2.15) high-angle shot – _____

_____

2.16) voice-over – _____

_____

2.17) sound effects – _____

_____

_____

_____

2.18) background music – _____

_____

_____

Check   Correct   Recheck

Commercial Activity

With your teacher's help, locate and view a school-appropriate commercial on the internet. As you view it, look for elements such as visual and audio techniques and graphic elements. Summarize the commercial below; then, answer the questions.

2.19) Summarize the commercial. _____

_____

_____

2.20) What product or idea is being advertised or promoted? _____

_____

2.21) What visual techniques and effects are used in the commercial? Describe them. _____

_____

_____

2.22) How do visual techniques enhance the message of the commercial? _____

_____

_____

2.23) What sound techniques are used in the commercial? Describe them. _____

_____

_____

_____

2.24) How do sound techniques enhance the message of the commercial? _____

_____

_____

2.25) What graphic elements does the commercial contain? (Hint: Does the commercial use an eye catching font to display text?) _____

_____

_____

2.26) Explain the overall message of the commercial. Is the commercial effective? _____

_____

_____

 **Teacher Check** ☐

3. THE INFLUENCE OF NEWS MEDIA

Objectives:

- Evaluate the role of media in focusing attention on events and informing opinion on issues.
- Evaluate various techniques used to create a point of view in media.

Vocabulary:

angle – the point of view from which a news story is written; slant

balanced – all sides of a story are presented equally and fairly

biased – one side is presented more negatively or favorably than the other

hidden agenda – a concealed reason or purpose for presenting information; having a bias toward one side of the issue

objectivity *[ob-jik-TIV-i-tee]* – a news story is balanced, not biased

Much of the information we obtain about the world and current events comes from the media. Unless we are eyewitnesses to an event, we must rely on others' accounts or the media to understand what's going on in the world. With so many media outlets—newspapers, magazines, television, radio, and the Internet— it is easy to access up-to-date information. With just the touch of a remote button or the click of a mouse, we can know what is going on all over the world almost instantly.

Since it is so simple to access information from a variety of sources, it is important to be discerning. Do all media sources tell the truth all the time? If information is printed in a newspaper or broadcast on the radio, does that make it true? No, in fact, even news media sources, which have the purpose of informing the public, can give false or misleading information. Although news sources aim to give accurate facts, news media sources are controlled by people who have opinions and

preferences. Sometimes, those opinions will be evident in the way information is presented.

As you learned in Lesson 1, the main purpose of news media is to inform the public of current events occurring around the world. A secondary purpose of news media could be to persuade the audience that an issue is important. By including an article about the dangerous effects of global warming, a newspaper is essentially saying that the issue of global warming is one that the public should be aware of and concerned about. News media sources decide what is important and inform the public about these issues. Often, the issues news media sources report are ones the general public should be aware of. Sometimes, however, news stories reflect the personal preferences of the news media sources.

Look at the following headline and subheading (from VOANews.com):

Film Explores Decline of Coral Reefs
Pollution, overfishing destroy 20 percent of world's reefs

Coral reef advertisement

You can tell from the headline that the article is about a film (documentary) that discusses the decay of coral reefs. Based on the news headline and subheading, it seems that the issue of the decline of coral reefs is one that the news media source thinks is important. The subheading uses the word *destroy,* which has a negative connotation. The headline is meant to arouse human interest, causing the readers to feel certain emotions.

All news stories are written from a particular **angle**, or point of view. Although the angle of a news story should be as neutral as possible, sometimes the angle is **biased**, presenting one side of the issue more favorably or negatively than the other. Consider the two newspaper

Newspaper headlines

headlines. They describe the same news story, but they represent different points of view.

The first headline states a statistic, a numerical fact that can be proven. It displays a neutral point of view. The second headline shows a negative slant against schools, portraying disapproval. Often, readers skim the headlines without reading the articles, so a headline that shows a negative slant could influence a reader's opinion about the issue. The second headline would likely cause a reader to have a negative opinion about the schools for failing to control student drop-outs. As you can see, different angles for the same story can influence readers' opinions in different ways.

BALANCED VS. BIASED

As you learned in Unit 8, Persuasive Writing and Speaking, a text that is biased shows evidence of a writer's strong opinion for or against an issue. In media, bias causes a source to present one side of an issue more favorably or negatively than the other side. Sometimes, news media sources have a **hidden agenda**, a concealed reason for reporting certain information. A hidden agenda is a source's private concern or goal, and it can often influence what kind of information the source presents. In contrast, a **balanced** text is one that presents all sides of an issue equally and fairly. It refrains from using rhetorical fallacies, such as caricatures, stereotypes, leading questions, and loaded language. A balanced news report does not leave out important information that would provide perspective on an issue.

A balanced media source shows **objectivity** by representing an issue in a neutral light. An objective source is one that does not display evidence of personal preferences or opinions. Instead, it presents a fair, honest view of both sides of an issue. Also, an objective source does not use words with strongly positive or negative connotations.

EVALUATING MEDIA BIAS

How can you determine if a media source is biased? The following indicators will help you recognize bias in a media source:

- Loaded language – Using words with strong positive or negative connotations indicates bias.
- Prevalence of opinions rather than facts – Including strong opinions without facts to back them up shows bias.
- Strong emotional appeals to pity and fear
- Rhetorical fallacies, such as stereotyping and leading questions
- Limited perspective – Presenting only one side of the issue indicates bias.

As you read, view, and listen to news media, make sure that you evaluate each source of information. Do not be influenced by media sources that show bias or a positive or negative angle on an issue. Obtain information from sources that are balanced and objective in their presentation of information.

Read the following article.

In The News

"Study: Eating Red Meat Increases Death Risk"
Consuming processed meats presents even greater danger

by Art Chimes
March 13, 2012

Eating red meat increases the risk of premature death, according to a new study, which also finds consuming processed meats presents an even greater risk.

The study tracked 120,000 Americans for up to 28 years, using data from two huge, ongoing studies of nurses and other health professionals. Their health is monitored and correlated with their living habits—including their diet.

"So, both processed and unprocessed red meat [were] associated with substantially increased risk of mortality," says Frank Hu of the Harvard School of Public Health, the study's senior author. "And clearly the risk associated with processed red meat is much higher than that for unprocessed red meat."

The researchers concluded that adding one 85-gram serving per day of unprocessed red meat, such as steak or hamburger, raised the risk of premature death by 13 percent.

Switch to a daily serving of processed meat—just two pieces of bacon or 28 grams of sausage, for example—and the risk goes up 20 percent.

In particular, eating red meat was linked to higher risk of death from cardiovascular disease and from cancer.

The study also found that substituting other foods for red meat—such as fish, poultry, and whole grains—could substantially cut the risk of premature death.

Although the study tracked participants for more than two decades in many cases, Hu says the impact of a change in diet can often be seen much sooner. "In most situations, dietary factors have immediate and short-term effects on cardiovascular risk factors and type 2 diabetes," Hu said. "So I don't think you have to wait for 20 years for the increased risk to occur."

The meat industry is taking issue with the findings.

Betsy Booren, director of Scientific Affairs for the American Meat Institute Foundation, criticizes the study's methodology, which included asking participants to remember how much meat they ate in the past.

Booren also points out that eating habits are only one of a number of factors that can affect disease and death.

"Many chronic diseases—cardiovascular disease, diabetes, cancer—the main risk factors are not food products," she says. "It's obesity, being overweight, and your genetics."

Hu's study did include a statistical adjustment for obesity and family history of disease, plus smoking, and found that red meat still contributed to premature death and disease.

Hu says his study doesn't mean that everyone should become a vegetarian, but that choosing alternative sources of protein may be a good idea.

"We found that other sources of protein, such as fish, poultry, nuts, legumes, and no-fat dairy products can have substantial benefits if they are used to replace red meat."

Answer the questions based on the previous article.

3.1) Look at the headline and subheading of the article. What kind of angle does the headline display? _____

_____

3.2) Is the article mostly based on facts or opinions? _____
Explain your answer. _____

_____

3.3) Does the article represent both sides of the issue? Explain._____

_____

_____

_____

3.4) Does the article leave out any information that might cause the reader to interpret the information differently? Explain. _____

_____

_____

3.5) How does the article seek to persuade the audience that this issue is important? _____

_____

_____

_____

3.6) Review the criteria for evaluating bias. Is the article biased? Explain. _____

_____

_____

3.7) What point of view seems to be recommended by the article? How do you know? _____

_____

_____

_____

Answer the questions.

3.8) What is objectivity, and why is it important in news media? _____

_____

_____

_____

3.9) What is the difference between balanced and biased news sources? _____

_____

_____

_____

3.10) What does "hidden agenda" mean in relation to news media? _____

_____

_____

_____

(Each answer, 5 points)
Match the techniques with the descriptions.

1.01) _____ high-angle shot

1.02) _____ low-angle shot

1.03) _____ close-up shot

1.04) _____ long shot

1.05) _____ camera angle

1.06) _____ special effects

1.07) _____ voice-over

1.08) _____ sound effects

1.09) _____ background music

1.010) _____ graphic elements

A. causes the subject to seem more threatening and imposing

B. headlines and sizes and styles of fonts

C. shows the subject and its surroundings, allowing the audience to see the "big picture"

D. the voice of an unseen narrator or commentator

E. makes the subject seem weak and vulnerable

F. the position of the camera while it is taking a shot

G. sets the mood of a scene and can affect the audience's feelings; enhances the action of a scene

H. allows the audience to see a person's facial expression

I. sounds added to films, television and radio programs, or commercials to entertain an audience and make the scene seem more realistic

J. computer-generated images and manipulated images that create an illusion

Choose the correct answers.

1.011) _____ Which of the following headlines shows a negative angle or slant?

    A. New restaurant provides employment opportunities for teenagers.

    B. Greasy burger joint encourages obesity epidemic.

    C. Citizens are concerned about unhealthy food served at Joe's Burgers.

    D. Joe's Burgers to open next Friday. Manager says burgers will be "on the house."

1.012) _____ Which of the following headlines shows a positive angle?

    A. Pollution levels decreasing thanks to city's new recycling initiative.

    B. Dingy, trash-littered streets show community's bleak future.

    C. Fish dying due to pollution in lakes and rivers.

    D. Mayor's recycling program faces opposition from the community.

1.013) _____ Which of the following articles would likely reflect bias?
   A. Canoeing in the great outdoors provides positive experience for teens.
   B. New park provides connection to nature in urban district.
   C. Deadly thunderstorms and tornados bring weekend to tragic end.
   D. Vegans protest harsh, unfair cruelty to animals.

1.014) _____ What is the target audience of a commercial for a cellular phone company that shows 13–18 year-olds having fun talking, texting, and surfing the internet on their cell phones?
   A. young children   C. teenagers
   B. parents   D. middle-aged adults

1.015) _____ Which of the following types of media has the primary purpose of entertaining an audience?
   A. newspaper   C. political campaign advertisement
   B. television sitcom   D. billboard advertising pet adoption

1.016) _____ Which of the following types of media has the primary purpose of persuading an audience?
   A. science magazine   C. commercial for a department store sale
   B. television talk show   D. radio news broadcast

1.017) _____ Which of the following types of media has the primary purpose of informing an audience?
   A. documentary   C. commercial for a Caribbean cruise
   B. political cartoon   D. animated movie

1.018) _____ Which of the following articles would be the most balanced and objective?
   A. an article that speaks against greed in big businesses
   B. an article in a school newspaper that calls for a "no homework" policy
   C. an article that discusses different viewpoints on an upcoming Presidential election
   D. an article that promotes a certain political candidate

1.019) _____ What is a hidden agenda?
   A. a stated reason for persuading an audience
   B. a strong opinion about an issue
   C. a viewpoint from which an article is written
   D. a concealed reason or purpose for promoting or speaking against a particular issue

1.020) _____ Which of the following statements about media is true?
   A. Media messages are intended to reach a large audience.
   B. Media messages are always persuasive.
   C. The main purpose of media messages is to inform.
   D. Media messages are usually fair and unbiased.

Check   **Correct**   **Recheck**

4. PROPAGANDA IN VISUAL MEDIA

Objectives:

- Evaluate the role of media in focusing attention on events and informing opinion on issues.
- Evaluate various techniques used to create a point of view in media.
- Evaluate the impact of media on the audience.
- Understand the use of propaganda techniques in media.

Vocabulary:

bandwagon – appeals to the audience's desire to be part of the crowd

card stacking – evading the truth by presenting only information that is positive toward an idea and leaving out negative information

glittering generalities – using words with positive connotations to portray a product or idea in a positive light

name calling – describing a person or idea using words with negative connotations

propaganda *[prop-uh-GAN-duh]* – writing or speaking that is intended to affect an audience's emotions in order to influence their ideas and opinions

plain folks – appealing to the needs, desires, and ideals of the "common man"

testimonial – using endorsements from well-known or respected individuals

transfer – using a symbol to attach a specific meaning to a person, product, or idea

In Unit 8 you learned about methods and techniques used for persuading an audience. Ideally, sound logic should be used to effectively persuade an audience. However, advertisements and other types of media normally use other methods. Sometimes, these methods involve using **propaganda** to influence an audience's emotions rather than their logical reasoning. Propaganda is writing or speaking that is intended to affect an audience's emotions in order to influence their ideas and opinions. Some ideas spread by propaganda are true; however, the aim of propaganda is to make an audience accept an idea whether it is true or false. Propaganda seeks to influence a reader or viewer's emotions rather than his or her mind, often using rhetorical fallacies, such as loaded terms and caricatures.

Some of the clearest examples of propaganda occur in posters, speeches, movies, cartoons, and other media of World Wars I and II. These media messages were intended to get the general public emotionally invested in the war. Wartime propaganda influenced the ideas and actions of the American people by persuading them to support the war financially, reinforcing negative ideas about the enemy, and encouraging the American people to "do their part" by working to support the cause.

Propaganda is commonly used in advertising to persuade an audience to purchase a product or accept an idea. Almost any commercial you see on television uses some form of propaganda to affect the emotions of the audience. Some advertisements cause the viewers to feel that purchasing a particular item will increase their popularity. Other advertisements appeal to viewers' feelings of fear, pity, love, or security.

What makes propaganda so effective? For one thing, it is more likely that a viewer will have an emotional response to a persuasive message than actually think about the ideas a message presents. Also, it is often easier for an advertising company to devise ways to evoke an emotional reaction from an audience than to present valid facts to persuade viewers. Often, viewers will be persuaded if they are caused to feel certain emotions, such as fear, pity, or desire to belong to a group. Understanding propaganda techniques used by advertisers will help you to be less easily persuaded by them.

PROPAGANDA TECHNIQUES

Media producers use several techniques to emotionally influence audiences. A media message will often employ more than one propaganda technique. Some techniques are very easy to recognize, while others require more attention to notice.

Bandwagon

Bandwagon propaganda appeals to the audience's desire to be part of the crowd. The main idea of bandwagon propaganda is, "Everyone's doing it, so you should, too." Its purpose is to make the audience feel that purchasing a product, accepting an idea, or participating in an action will bring popularity and acceptance.

When you analyze bandwagon propaganda, ask yourself if the idea is worth accepting, even if "millions" of other people have accepted it. Does the fact that so many people have purchased this product (or accepted this idea or participated in this action) make it worthwhile? Try to discern the true purpose behind the message.

Example 4.1

Example 4.1 is an advertisement for a 1966 Ambassador convertible "luxury car." It uses bandwagon propaganda as it appeals to young men to buy luxury cars because everyone else on their block is buying them. It appeals to the audience's desire to belong to the group by making the viewer feel singled out if he does not own the product advertised. The message is emphasized in the parentheses as the viewer is told to "hurry" and purchase the Ambassador.

Example 4.2

Glittering Generalities

Example 4.2 is an advertisement that attempted to persuade immigrants to support the war by purchasing war bonds. It uses words like *thrill, liberty,* and *duty* to represent positive ideas that the audience is supposed to associate with war bonds.

In **glittering generalities**, the media producer uses words with positive connotations to portray a product or idea in a positive light. Glittering generalities often include vague, emotionally appealing words like *love, freedom, justice, loyalty* and *honor*. Examples of glittering generalities in food advertising today include words and phrases such as *all-natural, pure,* and *organic.* The purpose of using glittering generalities is to get the audience to attach a positive idea with the product or idea presented. Glittering generalities are often found in advertising slogans, such as "Taste the rainbow" and "I'm loving it."

The soft drink advertisement in **Example 4.3** uses glittering generalities in the words *real taste.* The words are vague and are intended to appeal to the audience's emotions.

Example 4.3

Name Calling

Name calling involves describing a person or idea using words with negative connotations to try to get the audience to reject the person or idea without considering the facts of the issue. Name calling uses the rhetorical fallacy of *ad hominem*, attacking a person to present him in a negative light. Negative caricatures are also a form of name calling. Examples of name calling involve labeling a person as a *racist, Nazi,* or *Communist* in order to give others a negative opinion about him or her. A modern-day example of name calling occurs in a poster that compares those who download music illegally to Communists.

Example 4.4 is a World War II poster that uses name calling to reinforce a popular stereotype of that day of the Japanese. It was used to portray the Japanese in a negative light to influence Americans to work to support the cause of war.

FOR MURDER

Her careless talk costs lives

Example 4.5

Example 4.4

The poster in **Example 4.5** labels a woman as a murderer because it says her "careless talk" gave away secret and valuable information. The message is intended to serve as a warning to women who would be likely to gossip and share secret information about the war with those who do not support the American cause.

Card Stacking

Card stacking is a propaganda technique that involves evading the truth by presenting only information that is positive toward an idea and leaving out negative information. Card stacking propaganda uses carefully-selected evidence and purposely omits evidence that does not support the idea presented. An example of card stacking is an advertisement for a medical drug that lists all the benefits of the medicine but leaves out the negative side effects.

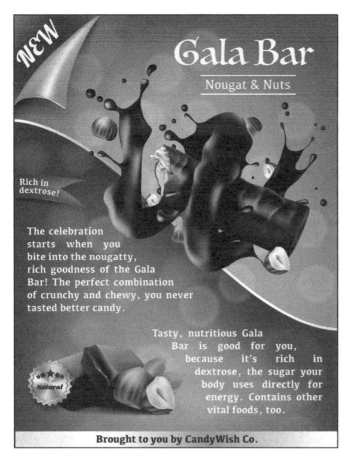

Example 4.6

The candy advertisement in **Example 4.6** uses a combination of card stacking and glittering generalities. It highlights the fact that the candy bar is "rich in dextrose" (sugar) and says that it contains other "vital foods." However, the advertisement does not mention that the candy bar is high in fat, especially saturated fat; instead, it claims that the candy bar is "good for you."

Plain Folks

The **plain folks** propaganda technique appeals to the needs, desires, and ideals of the "common man." Plain folks involves presenting ideas using common, ordinary language to gain the acceptance of the ordinary person. Another plain folks technique is a person portraying himself as a normal individual, just like everyone else, making him seem wise, wholesome, and good. A familiar example of plain folks is a picture of a political candidate shaking hands with normal people or eating in a "family" restaurant. In advertising, plain folks is often used to promote a product or idea by portraying an ideal American family.

In **Example 4.7**, an ideal American couple is used to promote the idea of war bonds. The underlying message is that if you purchase war bonds now, you will have your dream house in the future. It appeals to the needs and desires of the common American family.

Example 4.7

Transfer

The propaganda technique of **transfer** involves using a symbol to attach a specific meaning to a person, product, or idea. For example, a political advertisement that portrays a politician with an American flag waving in the background is using transfer to connect the idea of freedom with the politician. Transfer can be used to communicate positive or negative ideas. In addition to the American flag, common symbols used to transfer positive ideas include the cross, Uncle Sam, and the bald eagle.

Example 4.8 shows transfer propaganda by using a positive symbol, Uncle Sam, to promote the idea of buying war bonds. The idea implied by the poster is that buying war bonds is a way of advancing the cause of freedom.

The poster in **Example 4.9** uses transfer to portray a negative idea. The children in the picture are surrounded by a shadow of a swastika, the symbol of the Nazi regime. The overall message is similar to the previous example, except this poster takes a negative approach. It attaches the negative idea of Nazi influence with failing to purchase war bonds. Basically, the underlying message is that if you do not purchase war bonds, your children will fall prey to Nazi influence.

Don't Let That Shadow Touch Them
Buy WAR BONDS

Example 4.9

DON'T LET HIM DOWN !
Buy WAR BONDS
BACK UP OUR BATTLESKIES !

Example 4.8

Testimonial

The **testimonial** propaganda technique uses endorsements from well-known or respected individuals, such as celebrities, musicians, and athletes. Testimonial also involves using the opinions of a regular person to appeal to normal people. Often, companies will purchase the endorsement of a famous celebrity in an effort to entice consumers to purchase the product advertised. Testimonial can be misleading because, in many cases, the celebrity has never used the product and is only endorsing it for the money.

The advertisement in **Example 4.10** contains an endorsement for a product called Consoliderm that promises clearer skin. The customer who endorsed the product said

Example 4.10

that the product cleared her skin in just seven days. This statement may be true, but the results may not be the same for most people. This advertisement also uses glittering generalities to attempt to persuade the audience.

Appeal to Fear

Many types of propaganda use appeal to fear to convince an audience to accept or reject an idea or take a certain action. Appeal to fear is manipulating the emotions of an audience as a means of persuasion. This technique has been very effective in wartime propaganda, as it was used to convince Americans that unless they supported the cause of war, the country would fall under the influence of Nazism or Communism.

As you can see, propaganda can be very effective in influencing a person's emotions. Reading and viewing critically means evaluating explicit and underlying messages. Try to discern the influence of propaganda in media messages, and use your knowledge of the aims of propaganda to determine the validity of a message before accepting it.

These advertisements use appeal to fear to attempt to persuade the American people to support the war. **Example 4.11** is a poster that exploits Americans' fear of the Japanese during WWII to convince them to purchase war bonds. The image in **Example 4.12** is from the cover of a 1947 propaganda comic book. It uses fear-inspiring images to arouse anti-Communism sentiments.

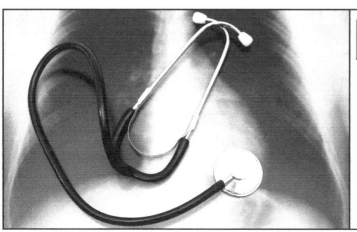

Pinpoint Problems

An x-ray machine and a stethoscope help medical doctors make a better diagnosis than they could with unaided sight, touch, and hearing.

Similarly, discernment allows a person to see beyond initial impressions and get to the root of a problem.

Example 4.11

Example 4.12

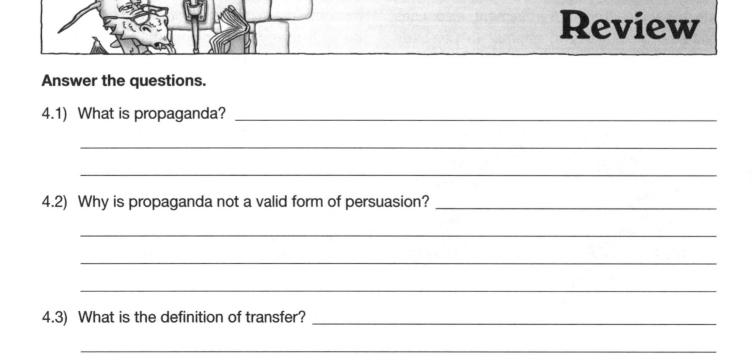

Review

Answer the questions.

4.1) What is propaganda? _____

_____

_____

4.2) Why is propaganda not a valid form of persuasion? _____

_____

_____

_____

4.3) What is the definition of transfer? _____

_____

Identify the types of propaganda using words from the box below.

appeal to fear	testimonial	plain folks
name calling	transfer	card stacking
bandwagon	glittering generalities	

4.4) _____ – describing a person or idea using words with negative connotations

4.5) _____ – appeals to the audience's desire to be part of the crowd

4.6) _____ – using a symbol to attach a specific meaning to a person, product, or idea

4.7) _____ – appealing to the needs, desires, and ideals of the "common man"

4.8) _____ – using endorsements from well-known or respected individuals

4.9) _____ – evading the truth by presenting only information that is positive toward an idea and leaving out negative information

4.10) _____ – using words with positive connotations to portray a product or idea in a positive light

4.11) _____ – manipulating the emotions of an audience as a means of persuasion

Identify the type(s) of propaganda used in each example.

4.12) a. _____

      b. _____

4.13) a. _____

      b. _____

Check   Correct   Recheck

5. EXAMINING MEDIA

Objectives:

- Understand the purposes of various types of media.
- Analyze how words, images, graphics, and sounds work together in various forms to impact meaning.
- Interpret how visual and sound techniques influence the message.
- Evaluate the role of media in focusing attention on events and informing opinion on issues.
- Evaluate various techniques used to create a point of view in media.
- Evaluate the impact of media on the audience.
- Understand the use of propaganda techniques in media.

Vocabulary:

deconstruct – to analyze the parts of something; to break down

media awareness – consciousness of the tactics used in media messages to influence audiences

So far in this Unit, you have learned about the various strategies media producers use to create messages for different purposes. The focus of this Lesson will be analyzing a variety of media messages to determine the impact of media on the intended audiences. This process is called **deconstruction**, breaking a message down into parts so that it can be analyzed. You will complete a **media awareness** project designed to help you be more conscious of the tactics used in media messages to influence audiences. Using your knowledge of media techniques, you will examine several different types of media messages and consider the methods used in each one to effectively influence an audience.

This project should be completed by the time you finish this Unit. You may work on the project during class, but you will need to spend time working on the project outside of school as well. Be sure to preview the project requirements and plan your time wisely. The media awareness project has three parts:

1 – analyzing media messages,
2 – summarizing the impact of media, and
3 – creating a media message.

All three parts will be evaluated in the final grade for this project. **The project will count as 50% of your Unit Test grade.**

MEDIA AWARENESS PROJECT GUIDELINES—OVERVIEW

Part One: Analyzing Media Messages

- Examine **ten** media messages, including at least one of each of the following: newspaper article, magazine article, print advertisement, billboard advertisement, television show, television commercial, and radio broadcast (news or human interest story).
  - For each media message, discuss the primary and secondary purposes, target audience, main idea/message, visual techniques, sound techniques, graphic elements, values/viewpoints implied, bias, propaganda, and impact on the audience.

Part Two: Summarizing the Impact of Media

- Based on the messages you examined in part one, summarize the impact of media on society.
- Write a three-paragraph response.
  - The first paragraph should introduce the topic and summarize the purposes and messages presented in media.
  - The second paragraph should discuss the underlying values and viewpoints presented in the media messages.
  - The third paragraph should summarize the impact of media messages on the intended audiences. Use examples from the media messages examined in part one.

Part Three: Creating a Media Message

- Create one media message promoting a product, person, or idea.
- The media message can be a print or billboard advertisement, a radio transcript, or a screenplay for a television commercial.
- Develop a clear message and viewpoint, and use visual and/or sound techniques to enhance the message presented.
- For a television or radio commercial, write a script/screenplay, including dialogue, stage directions, sound effects and music cues, and lighting and camera angle directions, as appropriate.
- On a separate page, explain the following techniques used in your created message: the purpose, target audience, message, visual and/or sound techniques, graphic elements, and values/viewpoints implied.

Technical Requirements:

- Create a booklet to present your findings. You may use construction paper as the front and back covers, and fill the booklet with several sheets of notebook or computer paper. Or, you may use a three-ring binder to keep the contents of the project together.

- Divide the booklet into three sections with a cover page for each section. You may use tabbed dividers or pieces of construction paper to mark the three sections.

- For part one, use a different page for each media message.

- Write neatly or type your analyses and summary. You may create your media message (part three) on the computer, or you may write/draw it by hand.

- Design a cover page that reflects the emphases of this Unit: types and purposes of media, techniques used in media, and bias and propaganda in media. Include the following information on the cover page: your name, the date, the Unit number, and class name.

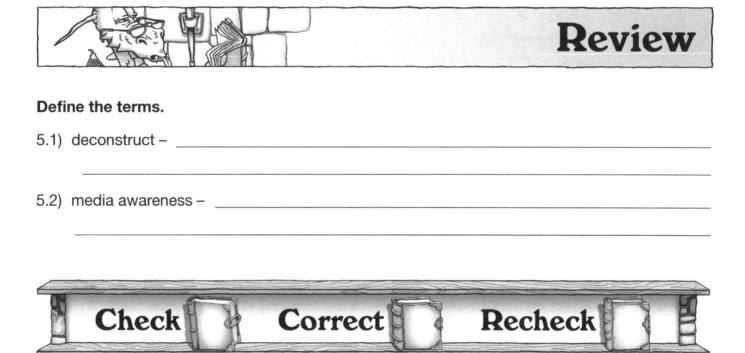

Review

Define the terms.

5.1) deconstruct – _____

_____

5.2) media awareness – _____

_____

Check   **Correct**   **Recheck**

EXAMPLE PART ONE ANALYSIS—FOLLOW THIS FORMAT:

Type of Media Message: television commercial

Company/Organization: The Shelter Project

Title/Subject: pet adoption

Description: An adopted cat observes a young boy playing in a sandbox, which the cat thinks is a giant litterbox.

Purposes: to persuade; to entertain

Target Audience: all ages, children and adults; people who like animals

Main Idea/Message: Pets are interesting and entertaining, so you should adopt one.

Visual Techniques:
- Close-up shot shows cat's expressions.
- Long shot shows cat inside and boy playing outside.
- Lighting draws attention to cat. Lighting is bright and cheery.

Sound Techniques:
- Voice-over (cat's voice) makes the cat seem humorous, intelligent, and human-like.
- Lack of sound effects and background music makes the audience focus on the cat's thoughts.

Graphic Elements:
- Slogan is displayed at the end of commercial - "A person is the best thing to happen to a shelter pet." The next shot displays, " BE THAT PERSON," along with the website for The Shelter Project.

Values/Viewpoints Implied: Pet adoption is important. You can provide a dog or cat with a better life through pet adoption. Adopting a pet will enrich your life.

Bias: The commercial is funded by a pet adoption organization, so it is biased toward pet adoption.

Propaganda: Glittering generalities in the slogan statement: " A person is the best thing . . . "

Impact on Audience: The commercial is amusing and makes me want to adopt a pet.

5.3) Complete the media awareness project, due at the end of the Unit.

Scoring Guide

Review the following project scoring guide carefully. Make sure that you meet all the requirements. **Remember, this project counts as 50% of your Unit Test score.**

Media Awareness Project Scoring Guide

Part One (50 Points) • Ten media messages analyzed. • All eight required types of messages included. • All elements included in analysis. • Explanations are detailed, complete, and show thoughtfulness.	_____/50
Part Two (20 points) • Summary includes three well-developed paragraphs. • Summary examines purposes, messages, values, viewpoints, and impact on audience of media messages. • Summary shows thoughtful reflection and analysis.	_____/20
Part Three (25 points) • Created media message follows directions. • Message and viewpoint are clear. • Media message shows creativity and thoughtfulness. • Reflection explains media techniques used.	_____/25
Format/Miscellaneous (5 points) • Booklet is neatly bound together. • Cover is illustrated with themes and ideas from the Unit. • Sections are indicated by dividers or cover pages. • Explanations are neatly written or typed.	_____/5
Total	_____/100

Teacher Check ☐

6. DIGITAL MEDIA

Objectives:

- Understand the purposes of various types of media.
- Analyze how words, images, graphics, and sounds work together in various forms to impact meaning.
- Interpret how visual and sound techniques influence the message.
- Evaluate various techniques used to create a point of view in media.
- Evaluate the impact of media on the audience.
- Assess the correct level of formality and tone for successful participation in digital media.

Vocabulary:

commercial – websites or web advertisements that have the purpose of persuading a user to purchase a product or support an idea

digital media – means of electronic communication that allow users to interact and communicate with other users, the device, or an application

educational/informational – websites that exist to give or explain information

formality – refers to the type of language and presentation used, as well as the rules of communication when participating in digital media

recreational – any site that has the purpose of providing enjoyment for users

THE ROLE OF DIGITAL MEDIA

Much of the information you take in every day likely comes from **digital media**. Digital media are means of electronic communication that allow users to interact and communicate with other users, the media device, or an application. Digital media include e-mails, text messages, websites, video games, web advertisements, and social media sites. If you have access to the Internet, it is likely that you use digital media more than any other type of media. With digital media, you can access information about current events minutes after they occur. You can look up a recipe without opening up a cookbook. You can communicate with a friend who is halfway across the world. You can purchase an item without leaving your home. You can look up information for a homework assignment without opening a book or encyclopedia. You can watch television shows, music videos, and video clips—whenever and wherever you want.

Digital media has made access to information quick and easy. By simply typing words into a search engine, you can access information almost instantaneously. Information can be stored and easily accessed on the Internet. Innovations in digital media have truly revolutionized the way our society receives and transmits information.

With all the ease and convenience of digital media, it is important for users to understand how to communicate effectively. This Lesson will discuss the various types and elements of digital media as well as guidelines for communicating effectively using digital media.

CATEGORIES OF DIGITAL MEDIA

Digital media can be divided into the following three categories:

- **Commercial** – Websites or web advertisements that have the purpose of persuading a user to purchase a product or support an idea. Websites maintained by businesses are also commercial websites.

- **Educational/Informational** – Websites that exist to give information are educational or informational. Educational websites are ones that give or explain information for the purpose of learning or teaching. Educational websites are often designed for students and include methods for students to practice what they've learned. Informational websites include news websites, how-to websites, online encyclopedias, and any other website that has the main purpose of providing information.

- **Recreational** – Recreational websites include gaming websites, social media sites, and any other site that has the purpose of providing enjoyment for users. Other forms of recreational digital media include text messaging, music applications, and instant messaging.

ELEMENTS OF DIGITAL MEDIA

Digital media differ from other types of media in that digital media allow users to participate in the communication. Digital media often combine elements of other types of media, including visual and sound techniques and graphic elements, adding the element of user participation. The amount and type of visual and sound elements a website uses depends on the type of website. For example, an educational website geared toward elementary students probably uses many exciting graphics and sounds to keep younger students engaged in the instruction. Similarly, recreational gaming websites use visual and sound techniques to make the games more exciting and to make users want to keep playing the games. Informational websites, such as news media

37

sites, tend to use fewer graphics in order to appear more professional.

The type of language and tone differs from one type of website to another. **Formality** refers to the type of language and presentation used, as well as the "rules" of communication when participating in the digital media form. Some websites, such as recreational websites, use more informal language. When interacting with other users on recreational websites, it is acceptable to use informal language and expression. A blog, for example, often uses informal language that has a personal tone, so when you communicate with others on a blog, you can use an informal, personal style of writing. Can you think of other types of digital media that use an informal tone and have more relaxed rules of communication?

Digital media that use formal language include informational websites, such as news websites, scholarly websites, business websites, and government websites. When communicating with more formal types of digital media, it is necessary to use a more formal and serious manner of expression. For example, if you want to write a response to an online news article, you should use a formal style and a serious tone so that other readers will take your response seriously.

Educational websites can use formal or informal language, depending on the audience. An educational website intended for high school or college students will use more formal language than one whose audience is elementary school students. Most educational websites use very precise language so that the concepts can be easily understood.

As you communicate using digital media, keep in mind that the style of language a website uses often dictates the degree of formality the user should use when communicating. Websites that use an abundance of graphics, visual techniques, and sounds are often less formal than ones that use fewer graphics and sounds.

In the activity for this Lesson, you will examine several different websites to compare and contrast the level of formality of each website, as well as the visual and sound techniques and graphics used.

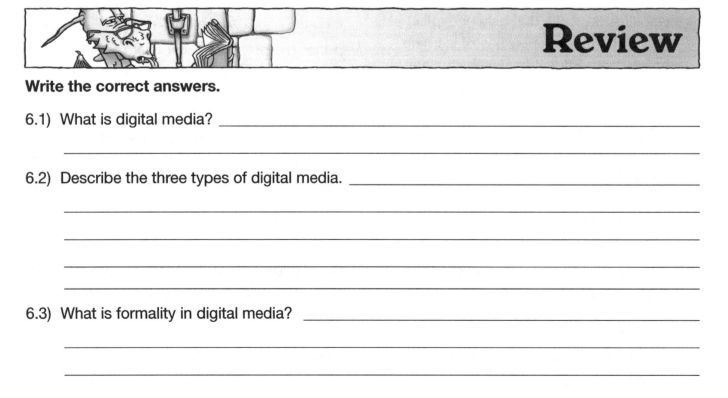

Review

Write the correct answers.

6.1) What is digital media? _____

_____

6.2) Describe the three types of digital media. _____

_____

_____

_____

_____

6.3) What is formality in digital media? _____

_____

_____

Match the words with the descriptions.

6.4) _____ commercial websites

6.5) _____ educational/informational websites

6.6) _____ recreational websites

A. purpose is to provide enjoyment for users

B. purpose is to persuade a user to purchase a product or support an idea

C. purpose is to give or explain information for learning or teaching

Check   Correct   Recheck

Activity

With your teacher's help, locate four websites: one commercial, one educational, one recreational, and one of your personal choice. After viewing each of the websites, fill in the following chart with information about the text, visual elements, sound elements, interactive elements, and the formality of each website.

6.7)

	Text: Summarize the content of the text and discuss word choice.	**Visual Elements:** Discuss the visuals, colors, graphics, shapes, and patterns used.	**Sound Elements:** Discuss any audio media used: music, sound effects, voice-overs, etc.	**Interactive Elements:** Discuss level of user participation.	**Formality and Tone:** Assess the formality and tone of the website.
Example (Educational) Name of Website: Funbrain	• Explains concepts in simple terms • Uses conversational language	• Bright colors • Exciting visuals (animals, cartoons) • Font makes text more appealing • Background pattern shows graphic of brain	• No sound effects, music, or voice-overs used	• Highly interactive website, including games to practice all areas of study	• Informal language, exciting tone • Appeals to younger children
Website #1 (Commercial) Name of Website:					

Website #2 (Educational/ Informational) Name of Website:					
Website #3 (Recreational) Name of Website:					
Website #4 (Choice) Name of Website:					

Answer the questions using information you gathered from the websites.

6.8) What relationship do you see between the amount and type of visual, sound, and interactive elements and the level of formality of websites? _____

_____

_____

6.9) Rank the websites you viewed from least formal to most formal.

a. _____

b. _____

c. _____

d. _____

6.10) How does the appropriate level of formality and tone differ across various websites? _____

_____

_____

6.11) What impact does the level of formality of a website have on the audience? _____

_____

_____

Teacher Check ☐

(Each answer, 5 points)
Match the words with the descriptions.

2.01) _____ propaganda

2.02) _____ deconstruct

2.03) _____ media awareness

2.04) _____ digital media

2.05) _____ formality

A. refers to the type of language and presentation used and the rules of communication

B. consciousness of the tactics used in media messages to influence audiences

C. means of electronic communication that allow users to interact and participate

D. writing or speaking that is intended to affect an audience's emotions in order to influence their ideas and opinions

E. to analyze the parts of something; to break down

Identify the type of propaganda in each statement using words from the box below.

bandwagon	card stacking	glittering generalities
name calling	plain folks	testimonial
transfer	appeal to fear	

2.06) _____ – Only a naïve, simple-minded fool would support this candidate's proposal.

2.07) _____ – Join the millions of Americans who are discovering the amazing results of Provita Juice every day. Call today for your one-month trial!

2.08) _____ – A famous athlete advertises a particular brand of energy bar.

2.09) _____ – Only pure, clear, natural spring water can taste this delicious!

2.010) _____ – Having grown up in a small town, I know what it's like to face economic struggles. Place your confidence in my plan, and I pledge to do my best to live up to my background as a hard-working individual.

2.011) _____ – A commercial for men's and women's jeans shows an American flag waving in the background and displays the slogan, "All-American Denim."

2.012) _____ – We can give you a great deal on that old clunker: double the rebate, financing, and even a free tank of gas. There are no bad parts to this deal!

2.013) _____ – Crime rates have been on the rise in your neighborhood. Install a TexaSafe security system today to safeguard your home against burglars, before it's too late.

Choose the correct answers.

2.014) _____ Which of the following is an example of a commercial website?
   A. a website that uses games to explain math concepts to students
   B. a website about the life and contributions of Abraham Lincoln
   C. a website that allows users to post pictures and comment on their friends' pictures
   D. a website that allows users to purchase clothing from an online store

2.015) _____ Which of the following is an example of an educational website?
   A. a website that sells sports equipment
   B. a website that teaches reading skills to elementary students
   C. a website for a wedding photography business
   D. a website that provides users with instant messaging capabilities

2.016) _____ Which of the following is an example of a recreational website?
   A. a government website that contains biographies of United States Presidents
   B. a website that explains the benefits of recycling
   C. a website that allows users to play games with one another online
   D. a website that helps students practice grammar concepts

2.017) _____ Which of the following websites would likely use the most formal language and presentation?
   A. a website for an online encyclopedia
   B. a social media site
   C. a personal blog
   D. a website that teaches history facts to elementary students

2.018) _____ Transfer involves the use of ___ to present an unrelated message.
   A. words   B. symbols   C. computers   D. foreign language

2.019) _____ Which of the following statements about propaganda is FALSE?
   A. The goal of propaganda is to make a person biased for or against something.
   B. Propaganda looks at both sides of the argument.
   C. Propaganda is everywhere—billboards, TV, radio, magazines, etc.
   D. Propaganda often uses emotionally loaded words to influence an audience.

2.020) _____ When attempting to persuade, speakers often use propaganda techniques. Propaganda techniques are ___.
   A. ways to organize your argument   C. ways to present facts clearly
   B. ways to manipulate your listeners   D. ways to create understanding in listeners

Check   **Correct**   **Recheck**

7. FORMAL AND INFORMAL SPEAKING AND LISTENING

Objectives:

- Use comprehension skills to listen attentively to others in formal and informal settings.
- Follow and give complex oral instructions to perform specific tasks, answer questions, or solve problems.
- Summarize formal and informal presentations.
- Speak clearly and to the point, using the conventions of language.
- Use eye contact, speaking rate, volume, enunciation, a variety of natural gestures, and conventions of language to communicate ideas effectively.

Vocabulary:

enunciate *[ih-NUHN-see-eyt]* – to pronounce words clearly and distinctly

gestures *[JES-cherz]* – hand movements used to emphasize key points

rate – speed

FORMAL VS. INFORMAL SPEAKING

In the last three Lessons of this Unit, we will discuss speaking and listening. You have done some public speaking this year. You have delivered a multimedia presentation and a persuasive speech. Both of those speeches could be classified as formal speaking. Any time you prepare remarks to present in front of a group of people, you are speaking formally. Formal speaking requires preparation. In delivering a formal speech, it is necessary to use correct grammar and to speak in a voice that can be easily understood.

When speaking formally, be sure to **enunciate** your words. Enunciate means to pronounce words clearly and distinctly. Also, speak at an appropriate **rate**, or speed. Do not rush through your speech. Use appropriate, natural **gestures**, or hand movements, to emphasize key points, and use expression in your voice when you speak. Finally, when giving an oral presentation, it is important to make eye contact with your audience. Doing so will help the audience to be much more engaged in your speech.

Informal speech, on the other hand, does not require preparation. You engage in informal speech every day of your life. Examples of informal speech include playful joking with your friends in between classes, comments or questions to your teacher during class, or conversations with your family around the dinner table. Many of the rules for formal speech also apply to informal speech, but in contrast with formal speech, informal speech is much more natural and spontaneous. In informal speech, it is not usually necessary to prepare what you will say beforehand. Informal speech usually involves more than one person, so it is important to listen carefully. Focus on what the other person has to say, and listen without interrupting. Give your opinion when it is appropriate to do so, but do not monopolize a conversation by not allowing the other person to speak. The most important rule in informal speech is to speak and listen politely.

PREPARING AN INSTRUCTIONAL SPEECH

You will practice formal speaking by delivering a formal instructional speech to a group of students. This speech is formal because you will prepare your remarks beforehand. An instructional speech (also known as a "how-to" speech) is one that guides listeners through steps in a process. With your teacher's guidance, you will deliver your speech to a small group of students, and you will instruct them on how to complete a certain task.

Informal speaking

Formal speaking

First, choose a topic for your instructional speech. This topic can be a task to complete, a problem to solve, or a question to answer based on a list of instructions. Select a process that you will be able to guide listeners through an oral explanation and demonstration, and make sure the process is one that can be completed in the classroom. You can demonstrate the steps for the audience as you explain them verbally, but your audience will not be able to read the instructions.

Once you have chosen an appropriate instructional speech topic, begin planning your speech. Make a list of materials that you and the audience will need. The process should use simple materials, ones that you can provide or ones that the audience already possesses. Then, make a list of steps in the process that you will explain to the audience. Use simple, understandable language, and be sure to clarify any unfamiliar terms for your audience. Use transition words that indicate the order of steps, such as *first*, *next*, *then*, and *last*.

Prepare for your instructional speech by filling out the following information.

7.1) Process (topic): _____

7.2) Materials needed:

    a. _____

    b. _____

    c. _____

    d. _____

7.3) Write clear directions for completing the process. Underline or highlight any words that you need to explain to the audience. Use transition words to introduce directions.

    a. _____

    b. _____

    c. _____

    d. _____

    e. _____

    f. _____

    g. _____

    h. _____

 **Teacher Check**

DELIVERING AN INSTRUCTIONAL SPEECH

Now that you have prepared your speech, it is time to deliver your instructional speech. Since it is a formal speech, you need to follow the formal speaking guidelines discussed at the beginning of this Lesson. Practice using correct grammar, enunciating your words, speaking at a normal rate, using appropriate gestures, and maintaining eye contact with your audience. When it is time to deliver your speech, make sure you come prepared with all the necessary materials. Explain the steps slowly enough so that your listeners can follow along. Use clear, simple language to explain the steps in the process.

7.4) **Deliver your instructional speech to a group of students.**

Grading criteria:

_____/20 The speaker used correct grammar when speaking to the audience.

_____/20 The speaker enunciated words and spoke at an appropriate rate and volume.

_____/20 The speaker used appropriate gestures and vocal expression.

_____/20 The speaker maintained eye contact with the audience.

_____/20 The speaker used clear, simple instructions to explain the process.

_____/100 total points

Teacher Check

FOLLOWING DIRECTIONS

Just as you have practiced giving directions, you will also practice following directions. In delivering instructions, it is the responsibility of the speaker to give clear directions, and it is the responsibility of the listener to listen attentively and follow the speaker's instructions. You will listen to an instructional speech given by a classmate, and you will perform the instructions described by the speaker.

As you listen attentively to the instructional speech, listen for verbal cues, or transition words that give the sequence of steps in a process. Give the speaker your full attention so that you do not misunderstand any steps. If you do not understand how to complete a step in the process, ask the speaker to repeat or clarify the instructions.

After you have listened to an instructional speech, summarize and evaluate the speaker's delivery.

Listen to an instructional speech; then, write your evaluation of the speaker's presentation.

7.5) What was the speaker's purpose? _____

_____

_____

_____

7.6) Summarize the content of the speaker's presentation. _____

_____

_____

_____

7.7) Evaluate the speaker's enunciation, rate, and volume. Could the speaker be easily heard and understood?_____

_____

_____

7.8) Comment on the speaker's use of gestures and vocal expression. _____

_____

_____

7.9) Did the speaker maintain appropriate eye contact with the audience? How did the speaker's eye contact enhance or detract from the delivery of the speech? _____

_____

_____

7.10) Evaluate the speaker's directions. Were they clear, simple, and easy to understand? _____

_____

_____

Teacher Check ☐

GIVING AN INFORMAL PRESENTATION

An informal presentation is one that does not require preparation. Rather than practiced and rehearsed, your speech should be spontaneous and natural. In a classroom setting, most of your presentations will be formal, but it is necessary to practice impromptu (unplanned, unrehearsed) speaking as well, as most of your interactions on a day-to-day basis are informal.

Informal presentations can be one-on-one or small group interactions. Often, informal presentations will involve audience interaction and free exchange of ideas. Informal presentations are characterized by a relaxed manner of delivery.

Choose one of the following options and deliver a two-minute informal speech to your teacher and a group of students.

☐ Describe a "pet peeve." Use examples and illustrations.

☐ Choose an ordinary item, such as a pencil, a roll of tape, a water bottle, or a notebook, and "sell" that item to your audience. Use your best persuasive skills to convince your audience to purchase that item.

☐ Describe your dream job.

☐ Explain to your audience why you would be a good candidate for President of the United States.

☐ Pretend you are a famous actor, athlete, or music artist. As that person, explain how you became so famous.

☐ Describe three things that you would change if you ruled the world.

7.11) Deliver an informal presentation to a small group of students.

Teacher Check

Summarize an informal speech given by a classmate.

7.12) Write a summary of an impromptu speech given by a classmate. Describe the topic and the speaker's delivery. Explain the elements that made the speech interesting, humorous, or unusual. _____

_____

_____

_____

_____

_____

Teacher Check

Review

Identify the following speeches as *formal* or *informal*.

7.13) _____ – Your teacher asks you to give a quick oral summary of last night's reading.

7.14) _____ – You deliver a speech explaining why you would be a good candidate for student council treasurer.

7.15) _____ – A high school valedictorian delivers a speech at graduation.

7.16) _____ – You explain to your parents why you have arrived home two hours late, covered head to toe in mud.

7.17) _____ – You present a slide show and give a prepared oral presentation to your classmates about your research topic.

Define the terms.

7.18) enunciate – _____

7.19) gestures – _____

7.20) rate – _____

Check   **Correct**   **Recheck**

STORY TIME

"Have you lost a camel?" asked the dervis.

"Yes," said the two merchants.

"Was he blind in his right eye and lame in his left leg?"

"He was," said the merchants, hoping the dervis had found their animal.

"Was he missing a front tooth, and did he carry honey on one side and corn on the other?"

"Yes," the second merchant replied, "can you tell us where he is?"

"I've never seen your camel," the dervis replied.

"By your description, you must have seen him," the merchants said. "What have you done with the gold?"

The merchants seized the dervis and brought him before a judge.

"I knew the camel had strayed because there were no human footprints along the course," said the dervis. "I knew the animal was blind in one eye because it ate the grass on one side of the path, and I saw the impression left by its lame foot in the sand. I saw he was missing a tooth because he left an uneven tuft in each bunch of grass. The ants told me it was corn on one side, and clusters of flies indicated the honey on the other."

- Would you have been able to tell that much about the missing camel?

- What can you observe around you now?

8. ADVOCATING A POSITION

Objectives:

- Speak clearly and to the point, using the conventions of language.
- Use eye contact, speaking rate, volume, enunciation, a variety of natural gestures, and conventions of language to communicate ideas effectively.
- Advocate a position using anecdotes, analogies, and/or illustrations.
- Work productively with others in teams.
- Participate productively in discussions, plan agendas with clear goals and deadlines, set time limits for speakers, take notes, and vote on key issues.

Vocabulary:

advocate *[AD-vuh-keyt]* – to support a specific position

constructive speech – a speech that gives arguments to advocate a position

debate – a public discussion in which teams present arguments for and against an issue

rebuttal – a speech that disproves or responds to the opposing viewpoint

DEBATING AN ISSUE

As we continue discussing and practicing public speaking, your tasks will become somewhat more complex. In previous assignments, you have given speeches that reflect your personal viewpoints. You have worked alone to deliver speeches. In the last two Lessons of this Unit, you will work cooperatively with two classmates to decide on a topic and key issues, plan an agenda, prepare speeches, and debate with another group of students.

A **debate** is a public discussion in which teams present arguments for and against an issue. For the debate activity, you will choose two debate partners and select another group of students to debate against. Each three-person team will debate either for or against

the issue. Your teacher may assign partners and teams.

Once you have formed teams, choose a topic to debate. The following list gives suggested topics. Choose one of the topics listed, or obtain your teacher's approval to debate a different topic.

TAKING SIDES

Once the two debate teams are finalized and the debate topic chosen, decide which team will argue for the issue and which team will argue against the issue. Using the first topic as an example, the "pro" team would argue that schools should ban junk food sales, and the "con" team would argue that schools should not ban junk food sales. Again, your teacher may assign you to argue for or against the issue.

DEBATE TOPICS:
- Schools should ban junk food sales.
- Cell phones should be allowed in schools.
- Television is a bad influence on children and teenagers.
- Zoos do more harm than good.
- Video games have a negative impact on children and teenagers.
- Social networking sites have a negative impact on society.
- Media advertising has a negative impact on society.
- Inappropriate content on the internet should be censored.

Perhaps you are trying to decide whether you are for or against the issue. Or, you may not have a choice of which side of the issue to advocate. Think about it this way— the focus of debate is **advocating**, or supporting, a specific position. The purpose of this activity is to be able to argue a position effectively. These issues are controversial, meaning there are good arguments for both sides of the issue. Even if you do not completely agree with the position you are advocating, work with your team to try to discern the best arguments to support the position.

List your teammates and write your topic/issue and position on the lines below.

8.1) Teammates:

    a. _____   b. _____

8.2) Topic/issue: _____

_____

8.3) My team's position on the topic/issue:

_____

_____

Teacher Check ☐

PLANNING AN AGENDA AND SETTING GOALS AND DEADLINES

Now that you have your teammates, topic, and position selected, it is time to begin working together as a group to plan your debate. The first step is to collaboratively (as a group) plan an agenda, or an outline for your debate. In a traditional debate, two individuals deliver a **constructive speech**, or a speech advocating your position. For example, the "pro" team would deliver two speeches, each giving a solid argument about why unhealthy snacks should be banned. The "con" team would deliver two speeches about why unhealthy snacks should not be banned. Constructive speeches will be three minutes long. In your agenda, decide which teammates will deliver constructive speeches.

The other speech in a debate is the **rebuttal**, a speech that disproves or responds to the opposing viewpoint. The rebuttal is delivered after each team has delivered two constructive speeches. During the debate, your team will take notes based on arguments presented by the opposing viewpoint and will respond to those arguments in the rebuttal. However, as a team, you should brainstorm arguments that the opposing viewpoint will present and plan to disprove them. Choose one teammate who will be responsible for delivering the rebuttal speech.

Speeches in a traditional debate are as follows:

- **First proposition constructive speech**
  The "pro" team delivers its first constructive speech, presenting a valid argument supporting the position. (3 minutes)
- **First opposition constructive speech**
  The "con" team delivers its first constructive speech, presenting a valid argument supporting the position. The first opposition speech can respond to arguments from the proposition. (3 minutes)

- **Second proposition constructive speech**
  The "pro" team delivers its second constructive speech, introducing a new argument and responding to arguments from the opposition. (3 minutes)
- **Second opposition constructive speech**
  The "con" team delivers its second constructive speech, introducing a new argument and responding to arguments from the proposition. (3 minutes)
- **Opposition rebuttal speech**
  The "con" team answers arguments given by the "pro" team and explains why

the opposition should win the debate. The rebuttal does not introduce new arguments. (2 minutes)

- **Proposition rebuttal speech**
  The "pro" team disproves and answers arguments given by the "con" team and explains why the proposition should win the debate. (2 minutes)

As you can see, each team will deliver three speeches—two constructive speeches and one rebuttal. Every team member will deliver a speech. As a team, decide which member will deliver each speech.

Next, set clear goals and deadlines for your team. Ask your teacher to give you a date for the debate, and decide when you will have your speeches written. You should have your speeches prepared at least one day before the debate so that you have time to discuss your ideas with your teammates and get feedback.

DISCUSSING IDEAS

Since this debate is a group project, you should spend time discussing ideas with your group. Before you begin writing speeches, hold a group discussion. As a group, decide the best arguments to support your position and brainstorm arguments to answer the opposing viewpoint. Every group member should take notes during group discussions. To decide on key arguments that support your position, you can take a vote in your group.

Record the results of your group discussion below.

8.4) Summarize the main points of your group discussion. _____

_____

_____

_____

_____

8.5) We determined that the best arguments to support our position are: _____

_____

_____

_____

_____ .

8.6) We decided that the best arguments to disprove the opposing viewpoint are: _____

_____

_____

_____

_____ .

Teacher Check ☐

PLANNING YOUR SPEECH

All the work until this point has been completed in a group setting. Now that you have determined what speech you are presenting and have gained helpful insight from your teammates for your arguments, it is time to begin writing your speech.

If you are giving a constructive speech, focus on developing specific arguments that support your position. Be sure that the arguments you develop in your speech are different from the arguments your teammate will develop in the other constructive speech. If you are delivering the rebuttal, make sure your speech answers and disproves the opposing viewpoint and explains why your team should win the debate. Do not develop any new arguments in the rebuttal. During the debate, the speaker delivering the rebuttal will make notes about key arguments presented by the opposing viewpoint, but it is important for the speaker to be prepared to answer those arguments.

As in the persuasive essay and speech, you need to use evidence to support your arguments. Your arguments will be much stronger if you have valid, relevant facts to back them up. You can also use real-life examples, anecdotes (stories), and illustrations to support your points.

Write a speech for your debate.

8.7) Write either a constructive speech or a rebuttal, depending on your assignment. Constructive speeches should be three minutes long, and rebuttals should be two minutes long. When you are finished, show your speech to your teacher.

Teacher Check

Fill in the blanks.

8.8) A(n) _____ is a public discussion in which teams present arguments for and against an issue.

8.9) To _____ a position means to support it with arguments and evidence.

8.10) A speech that gives arguments to advocate a position is a(n) _____ speech.

8.11) A speech that disproves or answers the opposing viewpoint

is a(n) _____.

Check **Correct** **Recheck**

FIVE KEYS TO DISCERNMENT

1 – Ask Why: When an injury requires surgery, trying to reduce the pain will no solve the whole problem. Similarly, surface problems can give clues to what is really occurring if you will stop, step back, and ask tough questions.

2 – Establish the Facts: Each person perceives a situation differently, and you must ask questions in order to find out what actually happened. Try to understand each person and gather as much evidence as possible before drawing a conclusion.

3 – Judge Carefully: Identify clues that indicate where a problem or a solution lies. Notice patterns, and pay close attention to details. Remember the timing of events does not always point to guilt. Weigh the facts carefully.

4 – Learn from Experience: Recall what others have taught you through their words and examples, and look back on your own experience to determine how you should respond to new situations.

5 – Act Appropriately: Knowledge only helps when you act upon it. Apply your knowledge to the circumstances at hand. Recognize what you need to start or stop doing.

9. PARTICIPATING IN A DEBATE

Objectives:

- Speak clearly and to the point, using the conventions of language.

- Use eye contact, speaking rate, volume, enunciation, a variety of natural gestures, and conventions of language to communicate ideas effectively.

- Advocate a position using anecdotes, analogies, and/or illustrations.

- Work productively with others in teams.

Vocabulary:

moderator *[MOD-uh-rey-ter]* – a person who acts as an authority over a debate or panel discussion

As a culminating project for this Unit, you and your teammates will participate in a debate with the opposing team. Your teacher will act as the **moderator**, or the authority in the debate or discussion. In a debate, the winning team is decided by which team presented the best arguments and most clearly disproved the opposing viewpoint's arguments. Your teacher will listen to the arguments presented on both sides and will decide which team wins the debate. A student who is not debating should be appointed as a time keeper to make sure that the speakers stay within the time limits.

Rules for a Debate

Speakers in a debate should...

- be prepared to speak
- listen to the opposing team's arguments and speeches
- be knowledgeable about the topic
- speak clearly and succinctly
- speak with enthusiasm
- support team members
- be polite to the opposing team
- speak within the given time limit
- follow the guidelines for formal speaking

Listeners in a debate should...

- remain quiet and be respectful of the speakers
- listen attentively
- take notes about key points in the debate
- evaluate the arguments and support given

Review

Define the term.

9.1) moderator – _____

_____

Check   Correct   Recheck

Using the remarks you have prepared, participate in a debate with the opposing team. When you are finished with the debate, answer the following self-reflection questions.

9.2) Which side won the debate? _____ Do you agree with the

decision? _____ Why or why not? _____

_____

_____

9.3) What do you think your team did well (list two things)?

a. _____

b. _____

9.4) In what areas do you think your team could improve?_____

_____

_____

9.5) What do you think the opposing team did well? _____

_____

_____

_____

9.6) In what areas could the opposing team improve? _____

_____

_____

_____

Teacher Check ☐

Listen to a debate presented by another group of students. Pay attention to the arguments and points each side gives. Complete the following graphic organizer with information about the debate.

9.7) Complete the graphic organizer, making notes about key points from each side of the debate. Write down reasons and evidence given to support points. Then, make a decision about which team won the debate.

Issue:			
PROPOSITION		**OPPOSITION**	
First Constructive Speech Speaker's Name:	Argument: Reasons/Evidence:	**First Constructive Speech** Speaker's Name:	Argument: Reasons/Evidence:
Second Constructive Speech Speaker's Name:	Argument: Reasons/Evidence:	**Second Constructive Speech** Speaker's Name:	Argument: Reasons/Evidence:
Rebuttal Speaker's Name:	Remarks to Answer Opposing Viewpoint:	**Rebuttal** Speaker's Name:	Remarks to Answer Opposing Viewpoint:
Winning Team: _____			

 **Teacher Check** ☐

(Each answer, 10 points)
Match the words with the descriptions.

3.01) _____ enunciate

3.02) _____ gestures

3.03) _____ rate

3.04) _____ advocate

3.05) _____ debate

3.06) _____ moderator

A. hand movements used to emphasize key points

B. a public discussion in which teams present arguments for and against an issue

C. a person who acts as an authority over a debate or panel discussion

D. to support a specific position

E. to pronounce words clearly and distinctly

F. speed

Choose the correct answers.

3.07) _____ A teacher who delivers an impromptu report about a recent fundraiser at a faculty meeting is giving a(n) ___.
    A. formal speech   C. constructive speech
    B. informal speech   D. rebuttal

3.08) _____ A speaker who disproves arguments by the opposing team in a debate is giving a(n) ___.
    A. formal speech   C. informal speech
    B. moderator   D. rebuttal

3.09) _____ A student who gives a prepared speech at the eighth grade awards ceremony is delivering a(n) ___.
    A. formal speech   C. debate
    B. informal speech   D. advocate

3.010) _____ In a debate, a speaker who presents arguments supporting his or her team's position is giving a(n) ___.
    A. moderator   C. constructive speech
    B. informal speech   D. gesture

Check   Correct   Recheck

STOP and prepare for the Unit Practice Test.

- Review the Objectives and Vocabulary for each Lesson.
- Reread each Lesson and its corresponding questions.
- Relearn each Lesson that you still do not understand.
- Review the Quizzes.

(Each answer, 2.5 points)

Match the words with the descriptions.

1) _____ target audience

2) _____ close-up shot

3) _____ high-angle shot

4) _____ long shot

5) _____ low-angle shot

6) _____ special effects

7) _____ visual techniques

8) _____ sound techniques

A. allows the audience to see a person's facial expression and helps create a certain emotion

B. elements such as camera angles and lighting that influence the message

C. makes the subject appear vulnerable or insignificant

D. computer-generated and manipulated images that create an illusion

E. makes the subject seem more imposing or threatening

F. sound effects, music, and voice-overs; used to enhance meaning

G. the specific group of people at which a media message is aimed

H. shows the subject and its surroundings

Choose the correct answers.

9) _____ Which of the following newspaper headlines shows a negative slant or angle?
   A. Community to implement bicycle sharing program.
   B. New fountain installed in Ramsey Park.
   C. Restaurant sued after seven contract food poisoning.
   D. Dirty, littered streets cast disapproving glare on city mayor.

10) _____ Which of the following indicates bias in a news article?
   A. stating the facts about the event or issue
   B. presenting only one side of an issue
   C. displaying a balanced view of a current event
   D. including an interview with a person involved in the event

11) _____ Which of the following websites is a commercial website?
   A. a website that explains basic camera techniques
   B. a website that allows users to compete against each other in games
   C. a website that sells crocheted hats and scarves
   D. a website that teaches users how to knit

12) _____ What makes digital media different from other forms of media?
- A. Digital media messages are usually persuasive.
- B. Digital media messages allow user interaction.
- C. Digital media use animated images.
- D. Digital media messages do not use visual and sound techniques.

13) _____ Which of the following types of media has the primary purpose of informing an audience?
- A. newspaper article
- B. social media website
- C. billboard advertisement
- D. feature film

14) _____ Which of the following types of digital media has the least formal language and rules of communication?
- A. a news media website
- B. an educational website for high school students
- C. a website for a political candidate
- D. a social media website that allows users to connect and communicate with friends

Fill in the blanks using words from the box below.

bandwagon	card stacking	glittering generalities
name calling	plain folks	testimonial
transfer	appeal to fear	propaganda

15) An advertisement appealing to the needs, desires, and ideals of the "common man" uses _____ to attempt to persuade the audience.

16) Stating only information that portrays an idea in a positive light is using _____.

17) Writing or speaking that is intended to affect an audience's emotions in order to influence their ideas and opinions is _____.

18) Displaying a symbol of freedom, such as an American flag, on a commercial for a political candidate is using _____ to get the audience to associate the idea of freedom with that candidate.

19) Packaging which describes a candy bar as "all-natural" and "low fat" is using _____ to convince an audience to purchase the candy.

20) "If you don't vote for this candidate, this country will probably turn into a Communist country" is a statement that uses _____.

21) Appealing to audiences to join the crowd or join the winning side is using _____.

22) An example of _____ is a commercial that uses a famous athlete to advertise a running shoe.

23) Using words with negative connotations to refer to a person is

_____.

Match the words with the descriptions.

24) _____ enunciate

25) _____ gestures

26) _____ rate

27) _____ deconstruct

28) _____ moderator

29) _____ debate

A. speed

B. to pronounce words clearly and distinctly

C. a person who acts as an authority over a debate or panel discussion

D. hand movements used to emphasize key points

E. a public discussion in which teams present arguments for and against an issue

F. to analyze the parts of something

Choose the correct answers.

30) _____ President John F. Kennedy's Inaugural Address is an example of a(n) ___.
   A. rebuttal
   B. informal speech
   C. constructive speech
   D. formal speech

31) _____ A speech that gives an argument supporting the position that smoking should be banned in public places is a(n) ___.
   A. constructive speech
   B. debate
   C. informal speech
   D. rebuttal

32) _____ A speech that disproves the argument that social media sites have a negative impact on teenagers is a(n) ___.
   A. informal speech
   B. rebuttal
   C. constructive speech
   D. debate

33) _____ An impromptu speech in which you share your opinion about the novel you are reading in your Language Arts class is an example of a(n) ___.
   A. debate
   B. rebuttal
   C. formal speech
   D. informal speech

34) _____ is a means of communication intended to reach a large audience.
    A. Media   C. Propaganda
    B. Formality   D. Moderator

35) _____ Writing or speaking that is intended to affect an audience's emotions in order to influence their ideas and opinions is called ___.
    A. media   C. propaganda
    B. formality   D. moderator

36) _____ is a type of language and presentation used; rules of communication in digital media.
    A. Media   C. Propaganda
    B. Formality   D. Moderator

37) _____ means that all sides of a story are presented equally and fairly.
    A. Biased   C. Slant
    B. Balanced   D. Deconstruct

38) _____ To analyze the parts of something and to break down is the definition of ___.
    A. biased   C. slant
    B. balanced   D. deconstruct

39) _____ A website whose purpose is to provide enjoyment for the users is called ___.
    A. recreational   C. commercial
    B. informational   D. educational

40) _____ is/are a means of electronic communication that allow users to interact and participate.
    A. Media awareness   C. Sound techniques
    B. Commercials   D. Digital media

Check   **Correct**   **Recheck**

You must now prepare for the Unit Test.

- Review the Objectives and Vocabulary for each Lesson.
- Reread each Lesson and its corresponding questions.
- Review and study the Quizzes and Unit Practice Test.

When you are ready, turn in your Unit and request your Unit Test.